WELCOME TO THE WORLD OF
Wild Cats

Diane Swanson

Whitecap Books
Vancouver / Toronto

Edited by Elizabeth McLean
Cover design by Steve Penner
Cover photograph by Thomas Kitchin/First Light
Interior design by Margaret Ng
Typeset by Tanya Lloyd
Photo credits: Chase Swift/First Light iv; Thomas Kitchin/First Light 2, 4, 6, 10,
14, 16, 20, 22, 26; Victoria Hurst/First Light 8, 12, 18; Daniel J. Cox/First Light 24

Printed and bound in Canada

Canadian Cataloguing in Publication Data

Swanson, Diane, 1944–
    Welcome to the world of wild cats

    Includes index.
    ISBN 1-55110-615-9

    1. Pumas—Juvenile literature. 2. Lynx—Juvenile literature. 3. Bobcat—
Juvenile literature. I. Title.
QL737.C23S92 1997   j599.75   C97-910657-5

The publisher acknowledges the support of the Canada Council for the Arts for
our publishing program and the Cultural Services Branch of the Government of
British Columbia in making this publication possible.

For more information on this series and other Whitecap Books titles,
visit our web site at www.whitecap.ca

Contents

World of Difference

SLEEK WILD CATS SLIP SILENTLY THROUGH THE NIGHT. Walking on their toes—claws in—they move nimbly, even crossing narrow ledges. When they spring, strong back legs power their high leaps. When they jump down, they swivel their bodies to land lightly on their feet.

Around the world, wild cats come in about three dozen kinds—lions, tigers, leopards, and more. In North America, there are three main cats: lynx, bobcats, and mountain lions. People call the mountain lion many names, such as cougar, puma, panther, deer tiger, painter, and catamount.

On the alert, the mountain lion watches for signs of prey and danger.

1

On snowshoe feet, the lynx runs quickly and easily across winter's blanket.

The mountain lion is the biggest cat in both Canada and the United States. It can stand as tall as a kitchen table and weigh more than 100 kilograms (220 pounds). That's about 10 times the weight of an average bobcat or small lynx.

Spotted as a kitten, the mountain lion grows a plain-colored coat as an adult.

Except for black trim on the face and tail tip, it's usually gray or reddish brown; sometimes nearly black or all white. But most bobcats have spotted or barred coats their whole lives. Even their short tails are marked with a black bar.

The longer, thicker fur of the lynx is often yellow-brown and spotted. Short, black fur tips its little tail and tall, black fur tips its ears. The lynx is a lanky, long-legged cat with big, furry feet—great for traveling in deep snow.

A long time ago, all cats were wild. Gradually, some kinds became tame—pets that lived with people. But pet cats that are left alone can turn wild again. They hunt for their food and raise their kittens as wild animals—just as lynx, bobcats, and mountain lions do.

These wild "pets," called feral cats, often live in cities: in parks, warehouses, and sewers. The males usually live alone. But the females may live in groups and raise their kittens together.

Where in the World

FORESTS, SWAMPS, AND GRASSLANDS. Wild cats claim homes, or territories, in several different kinds of land. Mountain lions often pick rough, rocky places. They live up high on mountain slopes and down low at sea level.

Some mountain lions and bobcats stay in dry, desertlike areas, where they blend right in. Others hang around soggy swamplands where there is plenty of water. Bobcats— like lynx—are very strong swimmers. Mountain lions can swim, too, but they prefer to jump across water. They can easily leap more than 4 metres (13 feet).

This bobcat blends with the colors of its rocky home.

Whenever it can, the mountain lion leaps over water to avoid swimming.

Many mountain lions, lynx, and bobcats live in or around forests. Lynx prefer thick woods for resting and for raising their families. But they usually hunt among bushes on land that has fewer trees.

The size of a wild cat's territory changes. If there's plenty of prey around, for example, cats claim small territories. But if prey is scarce, their territories can grow huge. The cats mark out the borders with their smell. A mountain lion scrapes up piles of dirt or leaves around its territory and adds its scent to them.

Today there are fewer wild cats than there once were. Mountain lions live mostly in western North America and in South America; lynx, across Alaska, Canada, the northern United States, and northern Europe and Asia; and bobcats, from southern Canada to Mexico.

TIGERS OF TIMES PAST

Slipping through tall grass, a saber-toothed tiger — bigger than a mountain lion — hunts for prey. It creeps close to a mammoth, then leaps. Grasping its prey tightly, the tiger drives two huge fangs deep into the mammoth's throat.

That's a scene from long ago. But the saber-toothed tiger hunts no more. Like the mammoth, it has disappeared. In all of North America, South America, and Europe, only its bones remain today.

7

World of the Hunter

A bobcat settles down to eat the day's catch: a ring-necked pheasant.

AS HUNTERS, CATS ARE MASTERS—built for catching prey. Their perky ears pick up soft sounds: the scampering of a squirrel; the high squeak of a mouse. Their big eyes let in lots of light to help them see in darkness. And moveable whiskers sense anything close—even without touching.

Surprise works well for these hunters. They pounce suddenly on prey, grabbing it with razor-sharp claws. Then they use their whiskers and long teeth to feel for the best place to bite—usually in the neck. One bite is often all they need.

When a wild cat feeds, its rough tongue

9

scrapes the meat off the bones. And the grooved roof of its mouth helps to grind up both skin and bones.

In North America, all wild cats catch small prey, such as mice, rabbits, and birds. A lynx prefers to eat snowshoe hares— rabbitlike animals with long

Mmm, porcupine! This mountain lion is going after lunch. It also hunts big prey, such as elk and bighorn sheep.

10

back legs and large feet. In fact, the more snowshoe hares there are, the more lynx move in to hunt them.

Now and then, a deer may become food for a lynx or a bobcat, but it's often prey for a mountain lion. As big as this cat is, it might take two or three weeks to eat a whole deer. The mountain lion might drag it nearly half a kilometre (a quarter of a mile) to find a good hiding spot. Sometimes it buries the deer under twigs and leaves until it's ready for another meal.

PICK A PRICKLY PORCUPINE

It may not be your choice, but a mountain lion might pick a porcupine for dinner. Tossing the creature — and all 30,000 quills — onto its back, the cat attacks the bare underparts and eats into the porcupine from there.

And those sharp quills? The mountain lion chews — and digests — some of them. A few may stick in its paws and face, but most fall out later. Quills that work their way under the cat's skin usually dissolve over time.

World of Words

LIVING ALONE, CATS DON'T TALK OFTEN. But when they must, they say a lot. They use sounds, signs, and actions to scare enemies and attract mates.

If people, wolves, or threatening cats come near, a wild cat might lean forward, twist its ears backward, bare its teeth, and hiss-s-s. Even a kitten hisses loudly at an enemy. A grown cat sometimes growls low and spits, too. It's all a way of saying, "Get lost."

When they speak, bobcats and lynx—the smaller cats—might try to make themselves look bigger and tougher. They stand

"I'm worried," this mountain lion is saying. When scared, it usually leaps into trees.

13

The lynx growls low and stares hard at another lynx, hoping to scare it away.

tall and raise their ears. Bobcats sometimes threaten by twisting their ears and showing the white spots on the backs of them.

An enemy cat might respond by flattening its ears and lowering its tail—even its whole body. Then it might slowly sneak away. "You win," it is saying.

When a wild cat looks for a mate, it

marks soil, bushes, and trees with smells from its saliva, urine, and body oils. These smells say who it is and announce that it's ready to mate. The cat might also leave mating signs by scratching the ground or trees around its territory.

Wild cats also speak to mates. The piercing screams of a female mountain lion carry her message a long way. But up close, wild cats meow, and they gurgle—like bubbling water—to say, "I'm friendly."

A PURR-R-FECT FEELING

"Pur-r-r-r, pur-r-r-r," says a kitten tucked close to its mother. It purrs as it sucks warm milk from her body. It purrs as it breathes in and breathes out. Purring is how a kitten says, "I'm feeling pur-r-r-fectly fine."

The wild cat mother purrs, too. The steady sound soothes her kittens. Purring is how she tells them, "All is well." It's not only comforting, it's a safe way to talk. Purrs are too soft for her enemies to hear.

New World

SPRING BRINGS MANY WILD KITTENS.
But new bobcats and mountain lions can
appear all year.

Wild cat mothers give birth in cozy
dens—sheltered spots inside caves, under
rock piles, beneath tree roots, or among
thick bushes. Two or more small kittens
usually arrive in each den. Even the
largest—the mountain lion kitten—weighs
no more than three or four bananas.

Newborns are helpless and need plenty
of care. They can't even open their eyes for
over a week. Their mother snuggles them
close. She keeps them warm and licks them

A bobcat kitten
feels safe near
its mother. Like
other wild cats,
it may live
about 15 years.

17

**This lynx kitten—
four weeks old—
waits among thick
bushes for its
mother to return.**

clean. She suckles them for hours at a time. If she moves much at all, the kittens cry.

Soon the mother must hunt to feed herself. Then the little cats stay in the den. They can crawl just a bit, so they nestle together to warm up—or wriggle apart to cool down. Their mother doesn't go far, and she returns to check them often.

Sometimes wild cat mothers have to change dens to keep their families safe. Grabbing loose skin at the back of the neck, the mother gently carries each kitten in her mouth. Even as adults, cats have loose skin, so they suffer less harm from bites.

For two months or more, wild kittens feed on their mother's milk. She gradually adds some meat to their meals until they no longer need her milk. Then it's time to teach the kittens how to catch their own food.

NO SITTER NEEDED

Hungry, the bobcat creeps from her cave. There is no one to watch her sleeping kittens. But no one is needed. Boulders hide the cave well. The cat has left her kittens there many nights before. In fact, this is the third family she has trusted to this den.

While she is gone, the kittens wake up. They're hungry, but they don't make a sound. Side by side, they wait by the cave's entrance, watching and listening for mom's return.

Small World

ROUGH TONGUES MAKE GOOD COMBS. Wild cat mothers use them to pull loose hairs and dirt from their kittens' soft coats. But grooming is just one of a mother's duties. The biggest job is teaching kittens how—and what—to hunt.

Lessons begin when a mother brings her prey to the den. At first, the kittens just watch her eat. Later, they start playing with their mother's dinner, and soon they're nibbling at it. One day, the mother brings her kittens some prey that is stunned or wounded. Then they practice pouncing.

Before long, the kittens are ready to go

Grooming two five-month-old kittens keeps this mountain lion mother busy.

hunting each night with their mother. They watch as she creeps close and leaps on her prey. They try to do the same.

All the while, the mother cat is watchful. Coyotes and other predators, such as eagles and big owls, might try to nab her young. If she senses danger, she growls. Then the kittens stand

Following a mountain lion mom in winter sometimes means getting a face full of snow.

like statues while she checks for trouble.

Wild kittens hunt with their mothers until they can live all on their own. For bobcats and lynx, that may only be about a year. But mountain lions stay with their mothers up to 20 months. They often hunt large prey, so they need more time with their mothers to practice their skills.

When it's time for the family to leave, the mother may shoo them away. The small, safe world of the wild kitten suddenly grows big.

When days are hot, wild cats know how to keep cool. They pant and they sweat—mostly through the pads of their feet. They nap in shade, stretching out to let their body heat escape. Sometimes they even lie down in water.

Cats also keep a cool head. Blood that travels through the skin in their noses loses heat, then flows to the base of the brain. This cooler blood picks up and carries away heat from blood that enters the brain.

Fun World

ANY TIME IS A GOOD TIME FOR
CAT PLAY. And here's a popular game:
One kitten flops down, tummy up. Its back
legs start "cycling," and its front legs slap
the air. A second kitten leaps beside the first
one and paws at it, furiously. Then, flip.
Flip. The kittens trade places, and the game
starts over again.

Wild kittens often play alone. They leap
at bushes, chase moths, and attack rolling
leaves. They play with dead—sometimes
live—prey, tossing it around. Games like
these help the cats judge distance and learn
when to strike. Play gives them a chance to

**Run! Pounce!
This mountain
lion is playing a
fast game that
builds good
hunting skills.**

25

practice their hunting skills.

Playing also gives kittens exercise that helps them grow healthy and strong. It teaches them to listen carefully, watch closely, and react fast when there's danger.

Wild cats play at all ages. Some adults play with each other before they mate.

A tiny bobcat practices tree-climbing through play.

26

Mother cats play with their kittens, wrestling, boxing, and grabbing their heads. In these scuffles, one furry body wraps around another and another. Then the kittens may break free and leap over their mother.

Like children, kittens play more than adults do. They play hard until they tire themselves out. When one kitten has had enough, it may jump into the air to signal the end of the game. Enough fun—for now.

WILD CAT WONDERS

Wild cats are wildly wonderful. Here are a few reasons why:

- The daggerlike teeth of ancient saber-toothed tigers were as long as the blade of a bread knife.
- When their whiskers brush against something, cats blink. That helps protect their eyes.
- Cats see well in just one-sixth the light that people need.
- Over 20 muscles swivel a cat's ear toward a soft sound.

Index